THE WORLD
IN THE TIME OF
ALBERT EINSTEIN

Belitha Press

FIONA MACDONALD

First published in the UK in 1998 by

Belitha Press Limited, London House, Great Eastern Wharf,
Parkgate Road, London SW11 4NQ

ISBN 1 85561 717 X

British Library Cataloguing in Publication Data
for this book is available from the British Library.

Editor: Christine Hatt
Series Editor: Claire Edwards
Designer: Jamie Asher
Series Designer: Roger Miller
Art Director: Helen James
Picture Researcher: Diana Morris
Consultant: Sallie Purkis

Printed in Hong Kong
9 8 7 6 5 4 3 2 1

Picture acknowledgements:
AKG London: 5b Erich Lessing, 6t, 6b, 7, 22b & 23 Dorothea Lange.
Bridgeman Art Library: 21t Private Collection, 33b Armoury Museum,
Kremlin, Moscow.
Camera Press: 25 A.Bailey.
Corbis Bettmann: 15.
E.T. Archive: back cover, 12, 28b Bakelite Museum, 29b, 37t Reina Sofia
Museum Madrid © Sucession Picasso Paris & DACS London 1998, 45b
Museum African & Oceanic Art, Paris.
Getty Images Ltd: front cover r, 5t, 16t, 17, 18, 24t, 26, 37b, 39t, 40,
44, 45t.
David King Collection: 43t.
Peter Newark's Pictures: 1, 2, 3, 4, 13t, 13b, 14t, 14b, 19t, 21b, 24b, 27tl,
27tc, 28c, 29t, 30t, 31, 32, 38t, 38b.
Norsk Sjøfartsmuseum Oslo: 33t.
North Wind Picture Archives: 19b, 27b.
Popperfoto: 22t, 42.

Picture acknowledgements contd.
Retrograph Archive Ltd, London: front cover l, 20, 30b, 34, 43b.
Spectrum Colour Library: 41b.
Trip: 41t D. Saunders.
Zefa: 16b, 28tr Heilman/Runk/Schoenberger.

CONTENTS

ABOUT THIS BOOK

This book tells the story of Albert Einstein, and looks at what was happening all around the world in his time. To help you find your way through the book, each chapter has been divided into seven sections. Each section describes a different part of the world, and is headed by a colour bar. As you look through a chapter, the colour bars tell you which areas you can read about in the text below. There is a history time line, to give you an outline of world events in Albert Einstein's time. There is also a science time line, which gives details of the major discoveries and inventions made during the same period. A world map shows some of the most important places mentioned in the book.

On pages 46–47 there is a glossary that explains some of the unfamiliar words used in this book.

THE STORY OF ALBERT EINSTEIN

▲ In this photograph, taken around 1950, Albert Einstein looks out with an enquiring gaze. Einstein won worldwide respect and admiration for his achievements as a scientist and his work for peace.

Albert Einstein was one of the most famous scientists who ever lived. He worked out a revolutionary new theory that completely changed the way scientists understand the world. It led to exciting discoveries in space, and helped other scientists to develop both deadly weapons and life-saving medical machines. Towards the end of his life, Einstein also became active in politics. This book tells you about his life as a scientist, and about his campaigns for justice and peace.

Albert Einstein lived from 1879 to 1955, a time of rapid change. There is no room in this book to describe everything that happened during Einstein's lifetime, but it will tell you about some of the most important events that shaped his world. Many of them still affect the way people live today.

◄ Albert Einstein, aged about five, and his sister Maja, dressed in the stiff, formal clothes that young children wore for 'best' in the late 1800s.

HONEST JOHN

Albert Einstein was born on 14 March 1879, in the city of Ulm, in southern Germany. His father, Hermann, was an engineer, who ran his own business. He brought Albert mathematical puzzles and scientific toys to play with at home – Albert preferred them to story books. Albert's mother, Pauline, was a housewife and a talented pianist. She taught Albert and his sister Maja to love music, and encouraged them to work hard at school. Albert did not enjoy school. He did not like its strict rules or organized games. But he did do extremely well in his mathematics lessons. His classmates gave him the nickname 'Honest John', because he was very hard-working.

COLLEGE LIFE

In 1896, when he was 17, Albert won a place to study science at a famous college in Switzerland. At the same time, he gave up his German citizenship. This was to avoid joining the army, which was compulsory for all German boys. Albert thought war was wicked. He was horrified at the thought that if he became a soldier, he might be ordered to shoot and kill people. For most of his life he was a pacifist, refusing to fight because he thought it was completely wrong.

A SCIENTIFIC CAREER

In 1900 Albert left college, and started to look for a job. For a while, he worked as a teacher, which he enjoyed. He also liked going to concerts, playing his violin, and spending evenings with friends in coffee shops, chatting, joking and discussing the latest scientific ideas. He fell in love with a young woman scientist called Mileva Maric. Later, they married and had two sons.

In 1902 Einstein was given a new job as an expert investigator, working for the Swiss government. His task was to check the claims made by inventors who wanted to register new designs. His scientific career had begun.

▼ The equipment-filled laboratory in the Technical High School, Zurich, Switzerland, where Albert Einstein taught from 1912 to 1914.

BUSY SCHEDULE

From 1905 to 1915, Einstein was very busy. He continued to study, and gave up his government job to become a university professor. He wrote many scientific papers and travelled to many countries. There he taught, met other scientists and campaigned for justice and world peace.

REVOLUTIONARY RELATIVITY

All this became possible because, in 1905, Einstein had worked out a revolutionary theory. It was called relativity, and provided a new way of measuring space, time and gravity, and of explaining how they work. It solved problems that had puzzled scientists for 200 years, and helped them to study the tiny atoms that make up matter. Using this new knowledge, they invented all kinds of devices, from weapons to machines for curing cancer. Einstein's theory also helped astronomers to discover amazing objects in space, such as quasars and black holes.

▲ Einstein teaching university students in the USA towards the end of his life. He was famous for his brilliant, eccentric lectures.

POPULAR PROFESSOR

At first only one professor understood Einstein's theory. But after Einstein published more papers on relativity in 1915, other scientists began to realize that it was true. Einstein became famous. In 1914 he returned to Germany to take up a post as Director of the Kaiser Wilhelm Institute, the top scientific job in the country. Throughout the 1920s, he was awarded prizes in many lands. He was also the world's favourite scientist – ordinary people liked him because he never became too proud and had a sense of humour.

◄ This photograph of Einstein sticking his tongue out at newspaper reporters was taken in the USA in 1951.

▲ Einstein (centre) taking part in an anti-war demonstration in Berlin, Germany, in 1923. The demonstration was organized by top scientists from many nations. Like Einstein himself, the world wanted peace.

RISE OF NAZISM

But Einstein's fame could not protect him from a new and terrible danger. In 1932 the Nazi party became powerful in Germany (see page 14). The party aimed to create a 'pure' German nation, by exterminating all the people that it thought were aliens, such as gypsies and Jews. Einstein was Jewish and a supporter of the Zionist movement, which campaigned for a Jewish homeland in Israel. He also bravely defended German Jews who protested against Nazi rule. After many threats and attacks, Einstein and his family were forced to flee from Germany. They left for the USA in 1933, and never set foot in Europe again.

LIFE IN THE USA

Americans were proud to welcome someone as clever as Einstein. So he was able to continue his teaching and research, and became a professor at Princeton University. He also joined in the fight against the Nazis by helping Americans to develop the world's first atomic bomb. This meant that Einstein had to abandon his pacifist views. But he believed that the Nazis were so evil, they had to be defeated at all costs.

A CHANGE OF HEART

Later, when Einstein saw the terrible devastation caused by atomic bombs (see page 14), he called for them to be banned. He also warned people against the dangers of uncontrolled science. He realized that dangerous experiments, scientific accidents or chemical pollution might one day destroy the whole world. By 1950 Einstein was seriously ill. But he continued with his scientific work, as well as his campaign for world peace. Einstein died in 1955, at the age of 76.

THE WORLD 1879–1955

ABOUT THE MAPS

The maps on this page will help you find
your way around the world in Albert
Einstein's time. The big map shows some
of the places mentioned in the text, including:

• **COUNTRIES**, as well as some important
states and regions.

• *Peoples*, such as the Mande.

• *GEOGRAPHICAL FEATURES*, including
mountains and rivers.

• *Towns and cities* To find the position of
a town or city, look for the name in the list
below then find the number on the map.

1	Pearl Harbor	8	Ulm	15	Amritsar
2	Hollywood	9	Berlin	16	Beijing
3	Chicago	10	Sarajevo	17	Shanghai
4	Lakehurst	11	St Petersburg	18	Vladivostok
5	New York	12	Moscow	19	Hiroshima
6	Guernica	13	Istanbul	20	Melbourne
7	London	14	Johannesburg	21	Sydney

The little map shows the world divided
into seven regions. The people who live there
are linked by customs, traditions, beliefs, or
simply by their environment. There are many
differences within each region, but the people
living there have more in common with each
other than with people who live elsewhere.
Each region is shown in a different colour –
the same colours are used in the headings
throughout the book.

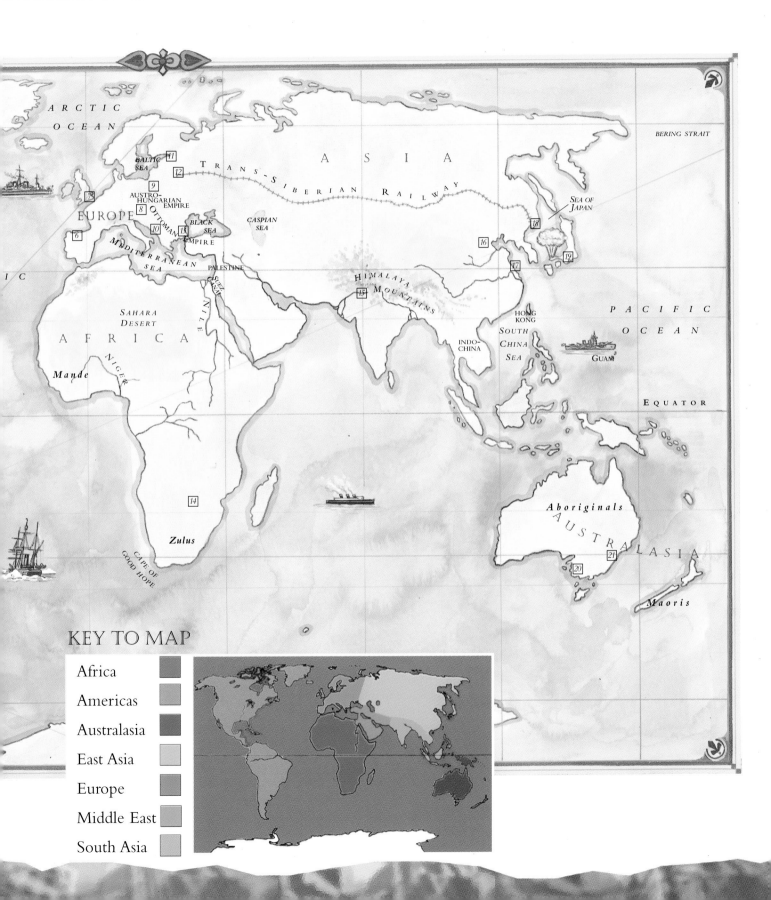

ARCTIC
OCEAN

A S I A

BERING STRAIT

BALTIC
SEA

11

12

T R A N S - S I B E R I A N   R A I L W A Y

SEA OF
JAPAN

9

7

AUSTRO-
HUNGARIAN
EMPIRE

8

EUROPE

OTTOMAN

18

CASPIAN
SEA

10

13

BLACK
SEA

6

EMPIRE

16

MEDITERRANEAN
SEA

SUEZ CANAL

PALESTINE

17

19

NILE

HIMALAYA

15

MOUNTAINS

SAHARA
DESERT

HONG
KONG

PACIFIC

AFRICA

SOUTH
CHINA
SEA

OCEAN

Mande

NIGER

INDO-
CHINA

GUAM

EQUATOR

14

Aboriginals

AUSTRALASIA

Zulus

21

CAPE OF
GOOD HOPE

20

Maoris

KEY TO MAP

Africa

Americas

Australasia

East Asia

Europe

Middle East

South Asia

TIME LINE

1875   **1890**   **1900**   **1910**   **1920**

EUROPE

1875-1898 First Labour Parties founded in many European lands.

1898 Germany plans to become world power. Builds new fleet and enlarges army.

1905 Rebellion in Russia. Tsar remains but agrees to some of rebels' demands.

1912-1913 Wars in Balkans (former Yugoslavia and nearby lands).

1914-1918 First World War.

1917 Successful Communist revolution in Russia. New nation (USSR) formed in 1922.

1919 League of Nations set up in Geneva, Switzerland to work for world peace.

AMERICAS

1885 Canadian Pacific Railroad linking east and west coasts completed.

1898 War between USA and Spain. USA takes over many former Spanish colonies, including Guam, Puerto Rico and the Philippines.

1910-1917 Mexican Revolution.

1912 Transatlantic liner *Titanic* sinks on first voyage.

1914 Panama Canal opens, linking the Atlantic and Pacific Oceans.

1917 USA joins in First World War against Germany.

MIDDLE EAST

1906 Rebellion in Persia (modern Iran) against rule of Ottoman Empire.

1907 Oil discovered in Persia.

1908 Young Turk revolution weakens Ottoman Empire.

1916-1918 Arab rebellions against Ottoman Empire.

1917 Balfour Declaration by British government promises Jewish people a homeland in Israel.

AFRICA

1875 Britain buys Suez Canal, Egypt.

1880-1881 First Boer War between Dutch farmers (Boers) and British settlers in South Africa.

1880s-1890s Britain, France, Belgium and Germany take part in 'scramble for Africa'.

1886 Gold discovered in South Africa.

1900 Copper mining starts in Katanga (part of the present-day Democratic Republic of Congo).

1899–1902 Second Boer War in South Africa.

1910 Union of South Africa formed.

1912 African National Congress set up by African leaders in South Africa.

1914 Britain takes control of Egypt.

1914-1915 Britain and France conquer German colonies in Africa.

1919 Successful rebellion in Egypt against British rule.

SOUTH ASIA

1876 Queen Victoria of Britain proclaimed Empress of India.

1879 Britain takes control of Afghanistan.

1885 Indian National Congress Party set up to campaign for independence from British rule.

1886 Britain takes control of Burma.

1906 Muslim League set up in India to campaign for independence from British rule.

1919 Peaceful protester killed by British troops Amritsar, India. Demar for independence incre

EAST ASIA

1894-1895 War between Japan and China. Japan wins some Chinese lands.

1898 Failed attempts at reform in China.

1900 Boxer Rebellion in China.

1904-1905 War between Japan and Russia. Japan wins.

1910 Japan takes control of Korea.

1911 Chinese Revolution. Until 1926, China is ruled by rival warlords.

AUSTRALASIA

1901 All separate states in Australia unite to become a single nation.

1898 USA takes control of Hawaii and Samoa.

1907 New Zealand becomes a dominion - a self-governing country within the British Commonwealth.

1915 Australia and New Zealand send troops to help Britain fight in First World War.

1930   **1940**   **1950**   **1955**

1921 Irish Free State breaks away from British rule.

1933 Hitler becomes Chancellor (head of government) in Germany.

1948 Communists (based in USSR) take over many Eastern European states.

1955 Military alliance of USSR and European Communist states known as Warsaw Pact set up.

1922 Benito Mussolini becomes leader of Italy.

1928 Stalin's first Five Year Plan to reform Russian farms.
1926 General Strike in Britain.

1936-1939 Spanish Civil War.

1942 Holocaust begins in Hitler's Germany.

1939-1945 Second World War.

1949 Military alliance of USA and non-Communist European states known as North Atlantic Treaty Organization (NATO) set up. Germany joins 1955.

1920-1933 Prohibition era in USA. Leads to increase in organized crime.

1933 US President Roosevelt begins New Deal welfare scheme.

1945 United Nations Organization founded, with headquarters in New York.

1947 Start of Cold War between USA and USSR.

1929 Wall Street Crash begins Great Depression in USA. This spreads to many parts of the world.

1941 USA joins in Second World War against Germany and Japan following Japanese air attack on Pearl Harbor, Hawaii.

1948 Marshall Plan gives economic aid to friendly European nations damaged by Second World War.

1950 McCarthyism - campaign against Communists in USA - begins.

1923-1924 End of Ottoman Empire. Atatürk sets up non-religious state in Turkey.
1925 Reza Khan becomes Shah (King) of Persia and introduces western-style reforms.

1932 Kingdom of Saudi Arabia set up.

1936 Oil discovered in Saudi Arabia.
1936 Arabs living in Palestine protest against arrival of Jewish immigrants.

1948 State of Israel set up. First Arab-Israeli War.

1926 Abd el Krim leads unsuccessful revolt against French rule in Morocco.

1939 South Africa joins in Second World War to fight against Germany.

1948 Apartheid introduced in South Africa.

1941-1943 Britain and Allies defeat Germans in North Africa.
1945 Unsuccessful revolt against French colonial rule in Algeria.

1952-1959 Mau-Mau rebellion in Kenya against British colonial rule.
1954-1962 War in Algeria against French colonial rule.

1928 Gandhi becomes leader of Indian National Congress.

1940 Indian Muslims demand separate state (Pakistan).

1947 India and Pakistan become independent from Britain.

1948 Gandhi assassinated.

1948 Burma and Ceylon (modern Sri Lanka) become independent from Britain.

1930 Gandhi leads protests against British Salt Tax.

1949 Indonesia becomes independent from Dutch rule.

1921 Chinese Communist Party formed.

1931 Japan conquers Manchuria.

1945 USA drops atomic bombs on two Japanese cities. Japan surrenders and Second World War ends.

1950-1953 Korean War between Communists and Nationalists.

1927 Chinese Nationalist leader Jiang Jie Shie begins fight against Communists.

1934 Mao Zhedong leads Chinese Communists on Long March.
1937 War begins between China and Japan.

1946-1949 Civil war in China between Nationalists and Communists. Communists win and set up new state.

1954 Laos, Cambodia and Vietnam gain independence from France.

1939 Australia and New Zealand join in Second World War to fight against Germany.

1951 Australia, New Zealand and USA sign a military alliance known as the ANZUS Pact.

1941 Japan attacks US fleet at Pearl Harbor, Hawaii.

1942 Battle of Midway (north of Hawaii). US navy stops Japan conquering more Pacific lands.

AROUND THE WORLD

In 1879, when Einstein was born, Europe was the world's most powerful region, with many overseas colonies, while the USA was growing richer and stronger. The Ottoman Empire ruled the Middle East, and ancient dynasties governed Russia and China. But by the end of Einstein's life, in 1955, many European countries had been devastated by two world wars, and had lost their colonies. The Middle East was divided among warring states, and Communist revolutions had transformed Russia and China. Two new superpowers, the USA and the USSR, ruled the world.

▲ During the First World War, soldiers fought in appalling conditions. This photograph, taken in France in 1916, shows a typical 'trench' – a tunnel dug in the mud where men ate, slept and sheltered from enemy gunfire.

ENEMIES AND ALLIES

EUROPE

European nations were jealous rivals. They envied each others' armies and navies, colonies, international trade and industrial wealth. Some countries, such as France and Germany, had a long history of mistrust and war. To support one another, rival groups of nations joined together in alliances. They agreed to defend their allies if any of them was attacked.

THE FIRST WORLD WAR

In 1914 this system of alliances finally led to war. In that year, Archduke Franz Ferdinand, heir to the throne of the Austro-Hungarian Empire, was shot dead in Sarajevo, Bosnia. His assassin was a Serbian, who wanted independence for Serbs in Austrian lands. So Austria declared war on Serbia, and Serbia's ally Russia declared war on Austria. Austria's ally Germany declared war on Russia in return. Soon most European countries were at war. Later, Australia, New Zealand, Canada and the USA joined Britain and France on the Russian side. The conflict became known as the First World War and lasted until 1918, when Austria, Germany and their allies surrendered. In 1919 governments set up the League of Nations, a society that worked to preserve world peace.

CIVIL WARS

In 1916 Ireland was under British rule. The Roman Catholic majority in the south wanted independence, but the Protestant majority in the north did not. Catholics rebelled against Britain in the Easter Rising of 1916, and in 1921 Ireland was divided. Six counties in the north remained British, while the south became self-governing. Civil war then broke out between rival groups in the south. In 1937 southern Ireland became the independent nation of Eire.

Civil war broke out in Spain in 1936 when General Francisco Franco overturned the elected government. He wanted to give power to the king and the army. After three years' fighting, Franco won. He remained in power until 1975.

▲ A dramatic painting showing Communist leader Lenin (top right) leading a protest march at the start of the Russian Revolution in 1917.

THE RUSSIAN REVOLUTION

Most Russians hated their cruel and inefficient government, which was headed by a royal ruler called the Tsar. They were angry because ordinary Russians were not allowed to elect its members. Russians also suffered terribly in the First World War. By 1917 many were sick and starving.

So, in March 1917, civilians and soldiers rioted in the capital, St Petersburg, and Tsar Nicholas II resigned. In November more riots broke out, this time organized by the Bolshevik Party, a Communist group led by Vladimir Lenin. The Bolsheviks executed the tsar and set up a government run by elected councils, called soviets. By 1921 the Communists controlled all Russian lands. They gave them a new name – the USSR (Union of Soviet Socialist Republics).

JOSEF STALIN

Lenin died in 1924 and a new Communist leader, Josef Stalin, took his place. He was an extremely cruel ruler, whose grand schemes often ended in disaster (see page 21). But he remained in power until his death in 1953.

▲ Nazi leader Adolf Hitler (centre) at a rally of supporters in Germany in 1933. He used mass meetings like this to stir up hatred against Jews.

THE RISE OF HITLER

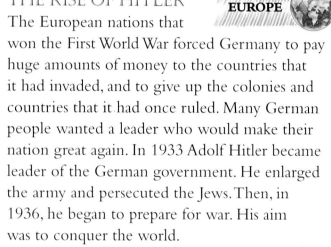

EUROPE

The European nations that won the First World War forced Germany to pay huge amounts of money to the countries that it had invaded, and to give up the colonies and countries that it had once ruled. Many German people wanted a leader who would make their nation great again. In 1933 Adolf Hitler became leader of the German government. He enlarged the army and persecuted the Jews. Then, in 1936, he began to prepare for war. His aim was to conquer the world.

THE SECOND WORLD WAR

Hitler was supported by Benito Mussolini, the dictator who ruled Italy, and by Francisco Franco, the army commander who ruled Spain. The government of Japan supported Hitler, too. But many other nations, including Britain and France, joined together to fight against him, and in 1939 the Second World War began. In 1941 Hitler tried to conquer Stalin's Russia. He failed, and the Russians became his enemies. In the same year Japanese aeroplanes bombed American warships in Pearl Harbor, Hawaii. This made the USA join in the war against Hitler, too.

THE POST-WAR WORLD

The Second World War ended in 1945, after an American aeroplane dropped the first atomic bomb on Hiroshima, Japan. Hitler killed himself, but many other Nazis were put on trial. Germany was divided up between the countries that had defeated it. One part was ruled by Communist Russia, the rest by Britain, the USA and France. Countries conquered by Germany and Japan were freed, but Russia took over many Eastern European states. To stop Communism spreading, the USA gave money and sent experts to rebuild Europe. To prevent more world wars, the United Nations Organization was set up in 1945.

▼ US 'Flying Fortresses' bomb Germany in 1944. The use of aircraft during the Second World War meant that, for the first time, whole cities were flattened and millions of ordinary people were killed.

NEW NATIONS

AMERICAS

For over 300 years, rival European nations had fought for control of land in North and South America. But by about 1900, almost all the new nations in the Americas had fixed their borders and become self-governing. Canada and Guiana, however, remained British colonies, and the Caribbean islands were still ruled by Britain, the Netherlands and France.

FIGHT FOR INDEPENDENCE

Most Native peoples in North America had lost their independence. Their last great – and unsuccessful – battle against European settlers took place in 1890 at Wounded Knee, South Dakota, USA. The South American rainforests were hard for settlers to reach, so Native peoples there continued their traditional ways of life. But their rights were not protected by law.

RISE OF THE USA

By 1900 the USA was the world's richest nation. At first, it concentrated on its own affairs. But soon it began to play a major part in international politics. It entered the First World War in 1917 (see page 13), and the Second World War in 1941 (see page 14).

COLD WAR

After the Second World War ended in 1945, the US government began to lead the fight against Communism in Russia and China. In 1949 the USA joined leading European nations to form the North Atlantic Treaty Organization (NATO). The aim of this military alliance was to defend the West against the Communist threat. Its establishment marked the beginning of a long period of high tension between the USA and the USSR known as the Cold War.

► Men of the Native American Comanche people were expert buffalo hunters and horse traders. In 1874 they were defeated by US forces and moved to a reservation in Oklahoma. This group of Comanche men, dressed in Western clothes, went to Washington D.C. in 1890 to discuss the return of their former homelands with the US government.

FALL OF THE OTTOMANS

MIDDLE EAST

In the 1870s, most of the Middle East was ruled by the Ottoman Empire from its capital city, Istanbul. By 1900 it faced threats from two strong neighbouring nations – Austria to the west and Russia to the north. Rebels from within the empire also challenged the Ottoman rulers. They wanted to reform the way imperial lands were run. In 1908 a group of army officers and politicians known as the Young Turks'rebelled against Sultan Abd ul-Hamid II, and removed him from power. Under their leadership, the Ottoman Empire fought on the German side in the First World War. The empire collapsed when Germany was defeated in 1918.

BIRTH OF ISRAEL

Once Ottoman power had gone, Britain and France were given mandates to maintain law and order in several Middle Eastern lands. Zionists (see page 44) claimed the right to a Jewish state in Palestine, a region under British control. This was difficult to achieve as many Christians and Muslims already lived there. A Jewish state, Israel, was created in part of Palestine in 1948, but Jews and non-Jews still quarrel over land there today.

▲ Zulu warriors in the late 1800s. They are wearing traditional feathered headdresses, holding wood and leather shields, and carrying spears called assegais.

SCRAMBLE FOR AFRICA

AFRICA

Until the late 1800s much of Africa was cut off from the rest of the world. But after European explorers brought back news of the continent's size and riches, European nations hurried to seize African lands. In 1884 a conference was held in Berlin, Germany. There, European governments took part in the 'scramble for Africa', dividing up large areas of African land among themselves. No one consulted African people. Their territories became colonies, and European farmers, miners and government officials settled on the best land.

◄ The flag of Israel, the nation created at the end of the Second World War as a homeland for Jewish people who had fled from Nazi persecution.

WAR AND REBELLION

There were many African rebellions against European powers. The Zulus fought the British in South Africa in 1879, and a Muslim religious leader, the Mahdi, fought them in the Sudan in 1885. In 1893, the Mande people of West Africa came into conflict with French settlers along the River Niger.

In South Africa, European settlers clashed with one another. From 1880 to 1881, and from 1899 to 1902, new British settlers and long-established Dutch farmers, known as Boers, fought each other. Britain defeated the Dutch in these Boer Wars, and in 1910 created a new nation, the Union of South Africa. It was independent, but linked to Britain both legally and politically.

▲ Workers at a South African gold mine in 1888. The discovery of diamonds in the country in 1867, and of gold in 1886, fuelled European interest in Africa as a whole.

TOWARDS INDEPENDENCE

North Africa was a battleground for European armies during the Second World War. When the war was over, nationalist leaders in many African countries began to demand independence from European rule. In 1945 there was an anti-French rebellion in Algeria. By 1954 it had turned into a war, and many French colonists were killed. Algeria finally achieved independence in 1962. In the British colony of Kenya, 'Mau-Mau' warriors attacked British settlers between 1952 and 1959. Kenya eventually became independent in 1963.

COLONIAL RICHES

SOUTH ASIA

European nations ruled many countries in South Asia. France claimed Indo-China (modern Cambodia, Laos and Vietnam), the Netherlands controlled Indonesia, and the British ruled Burma (modern Myanmar) and Malaya. Europeans wanted these lands for their crops, such as spices, coffee and rubber, and for their metals, such as tin.

JEWEL IN THE CROWN

India was the 'jewel in the crown' of the British Empire. But many Indians wanted to govern their own land. In 1885 the mainly Hindu Indian National Congress Party was founded to work for independence. In 1906 the Muslim League was set up to represent Muslims in the campaign.

▼ Indian independence campaigners face British soldiers during a march in Bombay in 1946.

TWO NATIONS

But Britain did not want to give India up. In 1919 British troops in Amritsar shot dead hundreds of Indians peacefully campaigning for independence. In 1942 the Congress launched a Quit India Movement, and warned that it might use violence. Faced with the threat of an uprising, Britain granted India independence in 1947. The land was divided into two nations: mainly Hindu India and mainly Muslim Pakistan.

SPREADING NATIONALISM

In the mid-twentieth century nationalists in other South Asian lands began to demand independence. From 1927 in Indonesia, and from 1946 in Indo-China, they rebelled against European rule. They were helped by soldiers hoping to copy Mao Zhedong's Communist revolution in China (see page 19). From 1948 Communists also fought the British in Malaya.

BOXER REBELLION

EAST ASIA

During the reign of Qing Empress Cixi (1862–1908), China faced many problems. Foreign nations, especially Russia, Britain and France, controlled its trade, and tried to take over its land. Japan attacked its north-eastern borders. Some Chinese leaders wanted to reform society by introducing Western science and technology. Others, including Cixi, hated all new ideas.

In 1898 the reformers seized power, but Cixi regained control. In 1900 gangs known as Boxers attacked foreign homes and businesses. Many foreigners were killed, but an army of Americans, Japanese and Europeans crushed this Boxer Rebellion. In 1911 the last Qing emperor, six-year-old Puyi, was removed from the throne. A republican government led by Sun Zhong Shan then began to rule the country.

▲ Mao Zhedong (left) after the 1934-35 Long March, during which Communists escaped from Japanese-controlled Chinese land.

PEOPLE'S REPUBLIC

Sun Zhong Shan soon quarrelled with other republican leaders and went into exile. But he returned to head a new government in 1924. From 1927 to 1937 China was torn by civil war between Sun's Republicans, the Revolutionary National Party, led by Jiang Jie Shie, and the Communist Party, led by Mao Zhedong. In 1937 the Japanese invaded the north. Supported by the USA and Mao's Communists, Jiang led the fight against Japan. But after Japan was defeated in 1945 (see page 14), the Communist Party won control of China. In 1949 Mao set up the People's Republic, based on Communist principles.

A NEW NATION

Australia and New Zealand changed rapidly during the late 1800s and early 1900s, as many new settlers arrived from Europe. The settlers felt patriotic about their new homelands. The first British governments to rule Australia had divided its vast territory into separate states, run as colonies. But by 1890, the states had won the right to govern themselves. In 1901 they joined together as a new nation, the Commonwealth of Australia.

Britain, Australia and New Zealand, which the British granted self-rule in 1907, were linked by sport, language and trade. Australian and New Zealand troops also fought to support Britain in both the First and Second World Wars.

ISLAND COMMUNITIES

Elsewhere in the Pacific, Britain, France, Australia and New Zealand began to rule islands that had once been independent. They hoped to make money from fishing or mining, or to use the islands' harbours for their long-distance ships.

In 1898 the USA took over Hawaii and Guam. Later these islands played a major part in the fight against Japan during the Second World War (see page 14). In 1959 Hawaii eventually became a state of the USA, and Guam still remains under US control.

► In both Australia and New Zealand, nineteenth-century European settlers built new towns like Adelaide (right) in European style, just like those 'back home'.

HOW PEOPLE LIVED

◀ Throughout the British Empire, everyone owed loyalty to the British monarch. If they could afford it, inhabitants of the empire were expected to purchase 'empire produce', such as British factory-made goods, Australian wool and Indian tea. This sweet tin was made to honour the British queen, Victoria. Behind her two portraits is a map of the vast British Empire.

During Einstein's lifetime, many people's lives changed dramatically. The greatest changes happened in Europe and the USA, and in the overseas colonies that European nations ruled. There, new mass-production techniques, farm machines and political ideas, as well as economic crises and the social upheavals caused by two world wars, meant that everyday life was never the same again.

European colonial rule over vast African and Asian empires, together with faster transport, better communications and increased trade, meant that, worldwide, people's lives were more closely linked than they had ever been before. But not all people living in European empires were equal. Almost all Europeans were richer, and lived in much better conditions, than the Native peoples in the lands that they ruled.

▲ British women in 1908, demanding the right to vote. Their campaign succeeded only after they had 'proved themselves' by doing men's jobs from 1914 to 1918.

WORKING WOMEN

EUROPE

The First World War caused many changes in the lives of European women. In the war they did many jobs that before had only been done by men, such as driving buses. Afterwards many still worked in these jobs because, at first, there was a shortage of skilled workers. (Almost 10 million men had died in the war.) Some people complained, but others viewed women with a new respect. Eventually women in most European countries were given the right to vote on equal terms with men.

ALL CHANGE

The war brought other changes, too. Many people no longer trusted the governments that had led them into such a terrible conflict. New political movements, such as Communism, attracted many followers. When Europe was affected by unemployment in the 1920s, then by the Great Depression in the 1930s (see page 22), there were riots and strikes. Many families left to make new lives in colonies overseas.

Joblessness and poverty led governments to develop 'welfare states' designed to provide pensions and free medical care for all. In Britain this new system was introduced in 1948.

STALIN'S SCHEMES

In the USSR Stalin planned grand projects to transform the country. He reorganized villages into huge 'collective farms' to mass-produce grain, and built vast steelworks and factories. Stalin made these plans from his headquarters in Moscow, without taking local people's advice. If they did not agree, he sent them to prison. Sometimes Stalin's schemes succeeded. But often they failed, causing pollution and starvation. Millions died in famines in 1920 and 1932.

▼ This Russian propaganda poster shows a worker in front of a new factory. His banner portrays Josef Stalin (left) and Vladimir Lenin.

AMERICAN DREAM

AMERICAS

In the late 1800s and early 1900s, American bankers, factory owners, oil well bosses and property dealers were famous for their know-how and tough talking worldwide. American skyscrapers, apartment blocks, factories, cattle ranches and farms were bigger than buildings and businesses in most other lands. Big cities were full of eager immigrants, all keen to work hard, make their fortune, and share in the 'American Dream'.

▼ By 1933, four years after the crash on the New York Stock Exchange, approximately 15 million people in the USA had no work. Many remained jobless for years. This was the depressing scene in a San Francisco unemployment office in 1938.

CITY CRIME

Two problems spoiled this picture of success. The first was crime. In the 1920s a new kind of criminal, known as gangsters, terrorized many American cities. Alcohol was banned in the USA during the 1920s, but gangsters ran bars where it was sold illegally. They also ran protection rackets, demanding money to 'protect' city businesses from crime. Business owners knew that if they did not pay, the gangsters would destroy their premises. Gangsters also took part in violent gangland wars, during which they murdered their rivals.

◄ Chicago policemen armed with machine guns fought to keep their city streets free of gangsters such as Al Capone.

GREAT DEPRESSION

The second problem was an economic crisis, known as the Great Depression. It started in 1929, when the New York Stock Exchange 'crashed'. Many businesses collapsed, savers lost their money, and millions of people became unemployed. In 1933 President Franklin D Roosevelt promised all Americans a 'New Deal' – a package of welfare benefits and laws. Life then improved for many in the USA, but the Great Depression continued to cause economic problems in many other countries.

▲ Many American families had
to leave their homes in the 1930s
when farmland turned to dust.

FARMING SUCCESS

Until the 1930s, farming boomed in many parts
of North and South America. The fast-growing
population of the USA, and its highly profitable
businesses, meant that food was in demand and
fetched high prices. Farmers in North America
cleared huge fields and bought high-powered
machines, like tractors and combine harvesters,
to help them work the land. They also started to
use chemical fertilizers to help them grow bigger
crops. In South America, farmers raised huge
herds of cattle, and tended vast plantations of
crops such as coffee, cotton and sugar.

FARMING FAILURE

But in the 1930s, American farmers became
poor. The Great Depression meant that they
could only get low prices for their produce. They
had no money to pay for food for their animals,
fuel for their machines, repairs for their buildings,
or rent for their land. Then, much of North
America was hit by another disaster. Low rainfall
caused the soil to dry up and turn to dust. High
winds blew it away, leaving just bare, stony
ground, where no crops would grow. Many
families were forced to abandon their farms
and move away in search of work.

FATHER OF THE TURKS

MIDDLE EAST

After the Ottoman Empire collapsed (see page 16), a new government came to power in Turkey in 1923. It was led by an army officer known as Kemal Atatürk, a name that means Father of the Turks. He was determined to set up a non-religious state, ruled by politicians rather than religious laws. Atatürk swept away old Muslim rules. He abolished writing based on Arabic script and replaced it with a new style that used European letters. He also introduced a new education system, new government officials, and new laws. Women were given political rights, and forbidden to wear the Muslim veil. Many new industries were introduced, too, in an attempt to make Turkey like the rich Western world.

▲ Oil was discovered in Persia (modern Iran) in 1907, and in Saudi Arabia in 1936. Soon oil pipelines and motor cars changed the desert way of life for ever.

OIL WEALTH

Many other nations in the Middle East kept their traditional Muslim customs and laws, but modernized their economy when oil was discovered. The first oil wells were drilled in Iran and Iraq soon after 1900, with the help of European technicians. Railways were also built, to carry drums of valuable oil to sea ports. For many people in Iran and Iraq, life after the discovery of oil remained much the same as it had always been. They continued to tend flocks of sheep and goats, or to grow crops in irrigated fields. But for others, oil wealth brought the chance of better housing and education, and of more contact with the wider world.

◄ Kemal Atatürk was the first president of the Turkish Republic. He is shown here wearing Western-style clothes, an example he urged all Turkish people to follow.

EUROPEAN COLONIES

AFRICA

For most of Einstein's lifetime, Africa was ruled by European nations. African colonies provided Europe with valuable raw materials, useful goods and wealth. Some colonies were also useful politically. For example, the Suez Canal in Egypt formed a vital sea link with India, Australia and New Zealand.

EUROPEAN EXPLOITATION

European colonial governments exploited their African colonies, sending profits from farms, ranches, gold and diamond mines back to Europe. African people did not benefit. Instead they worked hard for Europeans, growing crops or labouring in mines. A few European missionaries set up schools and hospitals for African people, but most Africans had little chance of good education or health care.

INTRODUCTION OF APARTHEID

Racism created great problems for many Africans, who did not have the same rights as European colonists. Racist attitudes were particularly extreme in South Africa. In 1948 the South African government introduced apartheid. This was a policy designed to separate black and white people, and to reserve all the best jobs, land, houses and education for whites.

▼ This bridge, in Cape Town, South Africa, was built in accordance with the country's apartheid laws. These were designed to keep people of different races apart. The bridge walkway is divided into two sections, one for whites, the other for non-whites. Anyone who walked down the 'wrong' side could be fined or even arrested and imprisoned.

THE RAJ

SOUTH ASIA

The British colony of India was governed by a huge civil service, led and trained by British men. Their families came to India to live with them, creating a rich, foreign ruling class, known as the Raj. Many members of the Raj made friends with their Indian workers, and with the Indian servants who cared for their children and ran their houses. But few regarded Indian people as their equals. The British relied on friendly Indian princes to help them rule. But they believed that ordinary Indians were not capable of running their country alone.

▼ A maharajah (prince) and his British and Indian guests at a tennis party in 1891. The setting is the city of Kapurthala in the north Indian region of the Punjab. There, many princes and ordinary people followed the Sikh religion.

INDIA'S ECONOMY

Many Indian people thought that Britain was damaging India's economy. Indians were not allowed to develop Western-style industries, in case they competed with British businesses. As a result, many Indian people were poor. Some worked hard producing cheap raw materials such as cotton, to be turned into cloth in Britain. Others grew crops such as tea for Europeans to consume. Many Indians moved to cities and took jobs as dockers, shopkeepers, cleaners or clerks.

MALAYA AND INDONESIA

The situation was very similar in many other European colonies in South Asia. In Malaya, large numbers of local people worked in European-owned rubber plantations, or as shipping clerks and servants. In Indonesia, they worked in coffee plantations or tin mines.

▲ A rich young noblewoman (left) and a poor peasant boy in China.

RICH AND POOR

EAST ASIA

A few Chinese people were very rich. They worked as top government officials, or as merchants at international ports such as Shanghai and Hong Kong. But most people in China were peasants, who worked very hard on their farms. Often, they barely managed to survive, and usually they were very poor. Sometimes crops died, or rival armies fought across their lands. Then there was famine, and millions of people starved to death.

COLLECTIVE FARMING

After Communist leaders won control of China in 1948, they took estates away from wealthy landlords and divided them among the peasants. They also killed about 2 million landlords for treating peasants badly in the past.

By 1950 about 650 million people lived in China. To produce more food to feed them all, Chinese leaders copied Stalin's plans (see page 21), introducing collective farming. Later, Chinese villages were encouraged to work together, and share all they owned. But this was not a success, and for a while, farm output fell.

► Sheep-shearers hard at work on a big Australian farm in 1891. Fine merino wool from Australian sheep was among the best in the world.

GROWTH AND CONFLICT

AUSTRALASIA

By 1890 Europeans in New Zealand and Australia had occupied almost all the land suitable for farming and mining. New towns also grew quickly. Melbourne in Australia had a population of 29,000 in 1851. By 1891 it was 473,000.

This rapid settlement led to disputes with local peoples. The Maoris of New Zealand fought the settlers fiercely and won the right to keep some of their ancient homelands. But many Maoris died in the fighting, and by 1896 only about 40,000 were still alive. In Australia, the situation was even worse. Whole Aboriginal communities died of hunger and European diseases.

FARM PRODUCE

During the early 1900s farmers in Australia and New Zealand were very successful. Refrigerated ships carried the meat, butter and cheese they produced to shops in Europe and many other lands. Top-quality Australian wool was also sold worldwide. But during the 1930s the farmers suffered badly. The Great Depression in the USA (see page 22) meant that people in other lands could no longer afford to buy their goods.

DISCOVERY AND INVENTION

During Einstein's lifetime, discoveries and inventions were made at an amazing rate. Some, like Einstein's theories, helped scientists to understand how the universe works. They were pure science – scientific study carried out to increase knowledge, rather than for practical purposes. Others, like televisions and jet aeroplanes, were very practical.

Many of the discoveries and inventions from this period had a greater effect than anyone could have imagined at first. Gradually, computers and antibiotic drugs, electricity and atomic research, have totally changed the way people live.

There is not enough room in this book to list all the inventions and discoveries that were made during Einstein's time. But you can read about some of the most important in this chapter, and find out about many more from the special science time line on pages 34-35.

▲ Penicillin, the first antibiotic drug, was discovered in 1928.

◀ A 1950 advertisement for the new Hawker 'Interceptor' jet fighter.

▼ A sturdy 1930s radio made from the early plastic Bakelite.

SPEED, CLIMB and RANGE

Extensive flight tests have proved the P1052 to have superior fighter characteristics. It combines high top speed and rate of climb with excellent handling qualities at all speeds and a range comparable with that of contemporary piston types.

HAWKER
P1052 INTERCEPTOR

HAWKER AIRCRAFT LIMITED

RADIO AND TELEVISION

EUROPE

Communications were changed for ever in 1901, when Italian inventor Guglielmo Marconi sent the first long-distance radio waves from Cornwall to Newfoundland. By the 1920s many Europeans had radio sets, and the BBC (British Broadcasting Corporation) made its first radio broadcasts in 1922. Scottish engineer John Logie Baird built the first television in 1926, but his design was replaced by a better version using technology invented by Russian Vladimir Zworykin in 1923.

TRANSPORT TRENDS

Until the late 1800s, nothing could move faster than a sailing ship. But by 1952, passenger jets could travel close to the speed of sound.

Among the most important transport inventions of this period were Gottlieb Daimler's petrol-burning internal combustion engine, motorcycle and early car, all made in Germany by 1885. The first bicycle was built in the same year. In 1888 Scotsman John Boyd Dunlop invented rubber tyres for bicycles. Later they were fitted to cars as well. Fast steam locomotives were also invented. The British *Mallard* reached almost 203 km/h in 1938.

► In 1906, British warship **HMS Dreadnought** was launched. It was one of the earliest steam turbine-powered ships.

► On 6 May 1937 the giant German airship *Hindenburg* crashed at Lakehurst, New Jersey, USA, after crossing the Atlantic. Thirty-three people died and many more were injured.

IN THE AIR

There were developments in air travel, too. French aviator Louis Blériot made the first flight across the English Channel in 1909, while British pioneers John Alcock and Arthur Brown made the first non-stop flight across the Atlantic in 1919. British aircraft engineer Frank Whittle invented the jet engine in 1930 and built the first jet aeroplane in 1937. Gas-filled airships were a popular way to travel until the terrible *Hindenburg* disaster of May 1937 (see above).

Russian scientist Konstantin Tsiolkovsky published designs for rockets between 1903 and 1913, though none was ever built. But by 1944, German rockets were so advanced that they were used to attack London in the Second World War.

LOUIS PASTEUR

Frenchman Louis Pasteur made one of the most important European breakthroughs in medical science. In 1880 he published his discovery that invisible germs – known as bacteria and viruses today – cause disease. He also found that these germs could be killed by heating. This heat treatment, called pasteurization, is still used to make milk safe. Pasteur also developed vaccines to protect humans and animals from diseases such as rabies.

X-RAYS AND ANTIBIOTICS

Wilhelm Röntgen, Marie Curie, and her husband Pierre, all investigated the X-rays given off by radioactive chemicals. Their discoveries made the modern uses of X-rays possible, such as the examination of broken bones, and the killing of faulty body cells that cause cancer and other diseases. In 1928 Scottish doctor Alexander Fleming discovered penicillin, a mould that kills bacteria. It became the first of many antibiotic drugs, which have been used to fight infections and save millions of lives worldwide.

▲ The research laboratory at Menlo Park, New Jersey, USA, where Thomas Edison invented the electric light bulb in 1879. He called the building his inventions factory.

INSTANT ELECTRICITY

AMERICAS

In 1879 American inventor Thomas Edison invented the electric light bulb. (In Britain Joseph Swan invented a similar bulb in exactly the same year.) Three years later, in 1882, Edison designed the first electricity-generating plant. It was built in London, but soon copied in the USA and other European countries. This allowed houses, streets, shops, offices and factories to have light and power at the flick of a switch.

MULTI-PURPOSE PLASTICS

In 1910 American inventors produced the first plastics. These materials could be used to make all kinds of objects, from boats and buildings to scientific instruments and sandwich wrappings. Synthetic fibres, like nylon, also had many uses. The first nylon stockings went on sale in the USA in 1940. Nylon was also used for parachutes to save airmen's lives in the Second World War.

▼ A 1946 American advertisement for rayon, one of the first artificial fibres.

◄ Model-T cars being mass-produced at the Ford factory, Detroit, USA, in 1925. Each car was exactly the same. Engineer Henry Ford once said that his customers could buy the cars 'in any colour they like – so long as it's black.'

CAR CULTURE

In 1913 motor car engineer Henry Ford designed the world's first production line for his factory, to make Model T cars. Parts for each car travelled down a conveyor belt. The workers stood alongside, each performing their own task. By the time the car reached the end of the production line, it was fully assembled and ready to drive. This way of making things was quicker and cheaper than old-fashioned craft techniques.

COMPUTER POWER

The first electronic computer was designed in Britain in 1943, and was used to break codes in wartime. It was secret, but the second electronic computer, the ENIAC, became famous. ENIAC was invented in the USA in 1946. It could do 5000 calculations per second, but filled a room. After engineers at the American Bell Telephone Corporation invented transistors in 1948, computers could be made much smaller.

TRAVEL AND TRANSPORT

Improvements in shipping made it easier for Americans to export foods and factory-made goods. The Panama Canal, completed in 1914, allowed cargo ships to sail from the Atlantic to the Pacific Ocean quickly, without making the long journey around the tip of South America.

In 1903 the world's first powered flight was made by American brothers Orville and Wilbur Wright. In 1927 American Charles Lindbergh made the first non-stop solo flight across the Atlantic Ocean. In 1947 Charles Yeager flew an American jet faster than the speed of sound.

FAST FOODS

Several new ways of selling and processing food were invented by Americans during this time. In 1916 the first self-service supermarket opened in the USA. After experiments in Alaska in 1925, Clarence Birdseye invented frozen food. In 1947 American shops began to sell microwave ovens.

► Jewish settlers using mules to plough the field of Armageddon in Israel in 1934. New farming methods enabled them to grow food crops in the desert.

DESERT FARMS

MIDDLE EAST

In the new state of Israel, the land was dry and rocky. From the 1940s onwards, settlers on communal farms called kibbutzim looked for new ways of farming that would 'make the desert bloom'. They drilled wells, dug irrigation ditches, and experimented with methods of removing salt from sea water to make it suitable for watering crops. Later, they also introduced new crops, such as avocados.

FARMS, MINES AND WELLS

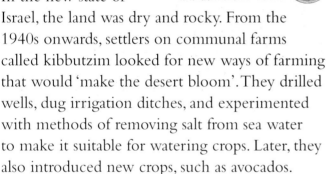
AFRICA

European farmers, hoping to get rich, introduced crops from abroad to African lands. But much greater wealth came from Africa's rich mineral deposits. The British explorer Cecil Rhodes discovered gold and diamonds in southern Africa in the late 1800s. People had known about the copper in Zambia and Zaire for centuries. But it was only in the early 1900s, when these countries were under European rule, that the minerals were mined in large quantities. Europeans organized the mining companies, but most of the dirty, dangerous work was done by badly paid Africans.

RAIL TRAVEL

Africa's first railways were built during Einstein's lifetime, mainly to help European farmers, ranchers and mine owners move their goods to sea ports for export around the world. One of the earliest was the Kenya to Uganda railroad in East Africa, which was completed in 1904. It also carried thousands of European settlers from the coast to their new homes inland. African and Indian labourers constructed this railroad. When it was eventually completed, most of the Indian workers returned to their homeland.

JAVA MAN

SOUTH ASIA

In 1859 British naturalist Charles Darwin had suggested that humans might be descended from apes. Since then, scholars had worked hard to discover if this was true. In the late 1800s and early 1900s, they set out on expeditions to remote places, hoping to find ancient human remains. In 1891 explorers on the island of Java, Indonesia, found bones from a creature they called Java Man. The bones did not come from a modern type of human, but from a human ancestor known as *homo erectus*.

JAPANESE SHIPBUILDERS

EAST ASIA

During the late 1800s and early 1900s Japanese politicians and businessmen were keen to learn about Western discoveries and inventions, and to introduce them to Japan. In the late 1800s they opened up many new ports to trade with Europe. Ships were the most important means of international travel, so the Japanese became expert shipbuilders, and Japanese companies owned some of the largest cargo-carrying fleets in the world. Japanese engineers also copied and improved Western railway technology – by 1906, a rail network had been built across their country.

TRANS-SIBERIAN RAILWAY

Even before the 1917 revolution (see page 13), Russia controlled many East Asian lands. The harbour at Vladivostok, on the coast of the Sea of Japan, gave Russian territories in Mongolia and Siberia an outlet for trade with these nations, especially Japan. In 1891 Russian engineers began to build the Trans-Siberian Railway. It was designed to link Vladivostok with Moscow, the biggest Russian city, far to the west. When completed in 1916, it was the world's longest railway.

► This gold model of a Trans-Siberian Railway train, and its egg container, were made by Peter Carl Fabergé.

▲ Roald Amundsen and his team stand beside the South Pole in 1911. Their huskies rest in the background.

ANTARCTIC EXPEDITIONS

AUSTRALASIA

In 1911 two rival expeditions left New Zealand with the aim of crossing the Antarctic ice cap to reach the South Pole. No one had ever made the journey before. Norwegian explorer Roald Amundsen carried tents and food on sleds pulled by huskies, reached the Pole quickly and returned in triumph. British explorer Robert Scott used ponies to carry his supplies, and took five weeks longer to reach the Pole. He died from cold, hunger and exhaustion on the return journey.

AIR TRAVEL

The invention of aircraft made it easier to travel to Australia, and to cross the vast distances within the country. In 1930 British pilot Amy Johnson flew to Australia on her own. Her flight was halted several times for repairs and took 19 days. But it encouraged other adventurers to travel by air. Within Australia, aircraft and two-way radios that used Morse Code made it possible to set up a flying doctor service in 1928. This brought medical care to the outback. Radios were also used to beam school lessons to children there.

SCIENCE TIME LINE

1879

The Eiffel Tower, Paris, France

885 Louis Pasteur (France) develops vaccine against rabies.

1889 Eiffel Tower, the world's tallest iron building, constructed in Paris, France.

1895 Wilhelm Röntgen (Germany) discovers X-rays.

1900

1900 Max Planck (Germany) formulates quantum theory, which helps to explain the structure of atoms.

1901 Guglielmo Marconi (Italy) transmits radio waves across the Atlantic Ocean.

1903 Orville Wright (USA) makes first flight in a powered aircraft.

1906 Roald Amundsen (Norway) makes journey through the North-West Passage, a route from the Atlantic to the Pacific Ocean, around the top of North America.

1914 Panama Canal completed, linking Atlantic and Pacific Oceans.

The Wright brothers' aeroplane

1920

1921 Albert Einstein (USA) wins Nobel Prize for Physics.

1923 Louis Victor de Broglie (France) publishes Wave-Particle Theory, which helps to explain how light and energy behave.

Alexander Fleming at work in his laboratory

1927 Charles Lindbergh (USA) makes first New York-Paris solo flight, in 33.5 hours.

1928 Alexander Fleming (Scotland) discovers penicillin, the world's first antibiotic.

1929 German airship makes first round-the-world flight.

1930

1930 Frank Whittle (Britain) patents gas turbine engine, used in 1937 to power jets.

1931 Auguste Piccard (Switzerland) makes first balloon flight into stratosphere.

1934 Ocean liner *Queen Mary* launched. Soon holds speed record for crossing the Atlantic Ocean in just under 4 days.

1935 Robert Watson-Watt (Scotland) invents radar system for navigation.

1938 Laszlo Bíró (Hungary) invents first usable ballpoint pen.

1939 Igor Sikorsky (USA) builds first helicopter.

1940

1943 Jacques Cousteau (France) invents aqualung for deep-sea diving.

1944 Germans use high-altitude V-2 rockets to attack London.

1945 USA drops world's first atomic bombs on Japan.

1947 Charles Yeager (USA) flies faster than the speed of sound.

1949 USSR explodes its first atomic bomb.

1950

Mount Everest

1952 British Comet becomes first passenger jet plane.

1953 Charles Townes (USA) invents maser, forerunner of laser.

1953 Edmund Hillary (New Zealand) and Tenzing Norgay (Nepal) make first climb of Everest, the highest mountain on Earth.

1954 Lawrence Seaway (USA-Canada) built, linking the Great Lakes to the Atlantic Ocean.

1954 First nuclear-powered submarine (USA).

1955

1955 Jonas Salk (USA) invents vaccine against polio.

1883   First skyscraper built, Chicago, USA.
1885   Gottlieb Daimler (Germany) builds first petrol-driven car.

1895   Lumière brothers (France) show first 'motion picture' (film).

1900   Sigmund Freud (Austria) publishes *The Interpretation of Dreams*, a pioneering book on how human minds work.
1903   Konstantin Tsiolkovsky (Russia) publishes first rocket design.
1903   The Flatiron Building, an early skyscraper, completed in New York, USA.
1909   Louis Blériot (France) makes first flight across English Channel.

1903   Marie Curie (Poland) and her husband Pierre (France) win Nobel Prize for their work investigating radioactivity.

1917   Karl Schwarzschild (Germany) publishes the black hole theory about mysterious, invisible areas of space.

Charlie Chaplin, one of the greatest stars of early 'talking pictures'

Charles Chaplin

1923   Vladimir Zworykin (Russia) invents first television tube.
1926   Robert Goddard (USA) builds first liquid-propelled rocket.

1926   John Logie Baird (Scotland) designs first television set.
1927   First 'talking picture' – film with sound (USA).

The Flatiron Building, New York, USA

1930   Paul Dirac (Britain) publishes Particle Theory. It helps scientists to understand how atoms are made.

1931   Karl Jansky pioneers radio astronomy (studying space by observing energy waves sent out by stars).

1935   Wallace Carothers (USA) invents nylon, the world's first 'test-tube' fibre.

1934   Charles Beebe (USA) dives 923 metres under the sea in a bathysphere, setting a new depth record.

1939   Paul Müller (Switzerland) invents chemical insecticide DDT.

1940   Britain's RAF pilots fly new Spitfire fighter planes to defend UK from German air attack.

1942   American rocket scientists build first nuclear reactor and produce first controlled atomic explosion.

A German V-2 rocket

1946   ENIAC computer built in USA.
1947   Dennis Gabor (USA) invents holograms.
1948   Bell Telephone engineers (USA) invent transistor.

1953   James Watson (USA) and Francis Crick (Britain) discover double helix structure of DNA, an important substance that carries genetic information in all living cells.

THE CREATIVE WORLD

FELIZ AÑO NUEVO

For thousands of years before Einstein, artists, musicians and architects in many lands had created works of art in distinctive local styles. Sometimes they borrowed ideas and techniques from distant countries, but their own special designs stayed basically the same. But by the end of Einstein's life, there had been a revolution in the arts. New media – cinema, radio, gramophone records and cheap colour printing – were carrying songs, dances, fashions and designs to a mass audience, worldwide. Styles just kept on changing, too, more and more quickly.

▶ This Spanish New Year card from the 1920s shows a fashionable young woman standing beside a gramophone. For the time, her clothes are very daring. Her dress is short, sleeveless, low-necked and loose around the waist. Her short hair is bobbed in the latest style.

◀ Pablo Picasso painted *Guernica* in 1937 to protest at the town's bombing in the Spanish Civil War.

▼ Russian ballet dancer Vaslav Nijinsky was famous for his dramatic style.

ART STYLES

EUROPE

All over Europe, painters were experimenting with new styles. Art no longer aimed to show people, places and objects as they really appeared. Instead, artists invented new ways of depicting ideas and feelings in their work. In France, Edouard Manet, Claude Monet and others painted in a dreamy style that used hazy blocks of colour instead of hard, sharp outlines. This was known as Impressionism. Other artists, like Spaniard Pablo Picasso and Frenchman Georges Braque, invented a new style of painting called Cubism. Cubist paintings showed objects from many different viewpoints all at once. Belgian René Magritte and Spaniard Salvador Dali were two of the most important Surrealist artists. They painted a strange, unreal world to shock people and make them think.

NEW DESIGNS

In Germany artists and craftworkers belonging to a college called the Bauhaus experimented with streamlined, industrial designs. In Britain sculptors like Henry Moore carved stone statues in curving shapes. French architect Le Corbusier designed the first high-rise block of flats.

MUSIC AND DANCE

There were also many new ideas in music and dance. Composers such as Arnold Schönberg, Benjamin Britten and Dmitri Shostakovitch experimented with a new musical scale. Claude Debussy attempted to create 'Impressionist' music – patterns of tones and moods. Igor Stravinsky caused a riot when his startling ballet music *The Rite of Spring* was first performed in Paris in 1913. Other new ballets caused outrage with their spiky movements. Nationalistic composers, such as Jean Sibelius of Finland, used legends and folk songs to inspire their work.

LITERARY LIFE

There were new trends in literature, too. Dramatists like Henrik Ibsen, Anton Chekhov and George Bernard Shaw wrote plays about real-life issues, such as poverty. English writers such as Wilfred Owen, horrified by the suffering of the First World War, wrote many poems and novels calling for peace.

POPULAR ENTERTAINMENT

The USA set the trends in popular entertainment. Hollywood was the world centre of film-making. Until 1927 most films were silent. But then talking pictures, known as 'talkies', began to draw vast crowds to cinemas.

From the 1920s to the 1940s, radio and gramophone records spread American music styles, such as jazz and blues, to many countries. American dances like the charleston, American dance tunes played by big bands, and American 'crooners' – glamorous soloists who sang in a romantic style – were also very popular. By the mid 1950s, American rock stars like Chuck Berry and Elvis Presley were famous everywhere.

▼ The Cotton Club, New York, USA, in the 1930s. The world's leading jazz musicians and dancers performed there.

▶ A souvenir postcard of New York's Chrysler Building, which was completed in 1930. It was decorated in ceramic tiles in the fashionable Art Deco style of the time.

MODERN ARCHITECTURE

American architecture was famous for its exciting new designs. In big cities like New York and Chicago, architects built skyscrapers made of steel, glass and concrete. They used the latest technology to make these structures taller and taller. The Empire State Building in New York was completed in 1931. At 449 metres, it was the tallest skyscraper ever built. American architect Frank Lloyd Wright won praise – and criticism – for designing stark, geometric buildings. They still influence many architects working today.

CRITICAL CARTOONS

In many Middle Eastern countries, art and politics were closely linked. Political cartoons in newspapers were very popular, and thousands were published between 1900 and the 1930s. They usually supported political reformers and opposed strict, old-fashioned governments, as well as interfering Europeans. Middle Eastern artists – especially in Turkey – also worked on huge propaganda posters and statues. These were designed to create a strong image for dynamic new rulers such as Kemal Atatürk.

▲ Dancers and musicians from the West African nation of Sierra Leone, photographed in about 1900. The masked man in the centre is a traditional healer.

TRADITIONAL DESIGNS

AFRICA

Throughout Africa, builders continued to create beautiful houses. Weavers, potters and woodcarvers carried on making fabrics, pottery, clay sculptures, masks and wooden statues in traditional designs. Some of these objects were used to decorate the homes of the rich, others were for religious use. African artists also used their skills to decorate European-style buildings, such as churches and hospitals. European colonial rulers built European-style cities. Among them was the gold-mining town of Johannesburg, South Africa, which was founded in 1886.

In Islamic countries of North and West Africa, mosques, schools and universities were built in a mixture of African and Middle Eastern styles.

AFRICA ABROAD

African achievements were admired by creative people in many other lands. In Europe, the Spanish painter and sculptor Pablo Picasso studied African carvings and masks, and copied them in many of his works. In the American South, where many African-Americans lived, traditional African music mingled with European music to create both the blues and jazz.

ANCIENT AND MODERN

SOUTH ASIA

In India, ancient themes were used in a modern way. Popular films, full of exciting battles, singing and dancing, retold ancient myths and legends. Industrial printing presses produced brightly coloured posters, showing gods and goddesses, saints and heroes, which ordinary people could use to decorate their homes. Craftworkers still produced the fine cloth that had made India famous for thousands of years. But now the thread that they used was factory-made, and the dyes contained chemicals, instead of plants and other natural materials.

EAST MEETS WEST

Easier, faster travel between continents, as well as international newspapers, magazines and radio programmes, made many Indian dancers, poets and musicians famous in Europe, the USA and beyond. Dancer Uday Shankar performed in Europe with leading ballerinas such as Anna Pavlova, and worked to preserve Indian traditional dances at home. Poet Rabindranath Tagore won the Nobel Prize for Literature in 1914, founded schools and a university, and travelled around the West giving lectures about Indian civilization.

JAVANESE ARTS

Many other traditional South Asian arts became well-known and admired in Western lands. These included dyed fabrics, known as batiks, from the Indonesian island of Java, and gamelan orchestras – groups of musicians playing bells and gongs.

▼ Dancers from the Indonesian island of Bali. Using elegant gestures, they tell ancient stories about gods and kings.

CHINESE ARTS AND CRAFTS

In China many expensive and beautiful art and craft objects were produced for Empress Cixi's court. They included jade vases, carved golden thrones, delicate flower paintings, glittering jewellery, silken carpets and magnificent embroidered robes. In 1888 a new Summer Palace was built north of the capital city, Beijing. The empress and her courtiers went there every year to escape the midsummer heat. The palace included a 25 metre-long, boat-shaped summerhouse in the middle of a lake. This was made of pure white marble.

After the Chinese royal family was overthrown in 1911, many of these beautiful objects were destroyed. For a time, while rival warlords fought to control China, new forms of art took their place. These included vivid propaganda posters and dramatic woodcuts showing battle scenes.

◄ Empress Cixi's Summer Palace, including the extraordinary boat-shaped summerhouse (left), was built using funds that were intended for modernizing the navy. The palace was damaged by European troops during the Boxer Rebellion of 1900, but restored three years later.

▲ When it opened in 1932, Sydney Harbour Bridge was greatly admired because its design combined technical skill with artistic flair. The tall pillars at each end of the bridge were intended to look like 1930s-style skyscrapers.

EUROPEAN TRADITIONS

AUSTRALASIA

When European settlers arrived in Australia, New Zealand and some Pacific islands, they brought their own cultural traditions with them. For many years, local Australasian music, stories, legends, arts and crafts were ignored or despised, while farms, schools, churches and homes were built to European designs. Some of these buildings were very impressive, for example the splendid, 503-metre-wide Sydney Harbour Bridge, which was completed in 1932.

CHANGING ATTITUDES

Aboriginal artists in Australia and Maori craftworkers in New Zealand continued to produce work in traditional styles, but it was not appreciated by many people, either at home or abroad. But from around 1950, attitudes began to change. Led by painter Sidney Nolan, Australian artists whose ancestors had come from Europe began to paint pictures that were inspired by Australian history and the magnificent Australian landscape. Meanwhile, scholars began to understand the important part traditional paintings, carvings, stories, dances and songs played in both Aboriginal and Maori life.

BELIEFS AND IDEAS

During Einstein's lifetime, traditional beliefs in many parts of the world were challenged and often replaced by new, non-religious ideas. The more scientific discoveries were made, the more they seemed to explain away the mysteries of the universe, and remove people's need to believe in an all-powerful God. But after Einstein's Theory of Relativity was published, many people felt that nothing was certain, not even rational scientific beliefs. They preferred to put their trust in individual human feelings, or in practical political ideas.

▲ When the first ever atomic bomb was dropped on Hiroshima, Japan, in 1945, people were astonished – and alarmed – by its power. They quickly realized that humans now had the means to destroy the Earth.

► The emblem of the USSR. It is decorated with a hammer and a sickle – symbols of workers' power.

RELIGIOUS DECLINE

EUROPE

In Christian Europe, the political revolutions and social upheavals of the 1920s and 1930s (see pages 12-14) shook people's beliefs. Many became atheists. Others joined political groups, such as the Communist Party.

Many organizations tried to fill the gap left by religion. People shocked at the suffering caused by wars, floods and famines set up societies to care for their victims. After the First World War, international organizations like the League of Nations were established to work for peace. The Eastern beliefs of Hinduism and Buddhism also became popular in Europe at this time.

LAND OF THE FREE

AMERICAS

In 1886 a huge steel and concrete statue of a woman carrying a flaming torch was set up on an island at the entrance to New York harbour. This was the Statue of Liberty. Liberty means freedom, and American people believed that their country was 'the land of the free'. People living there – including the millions of immigrants who had arrived in the late 1800s and early 1900s – were free to follow their own religions and make their own laws. They could also express their thoughts openly, because they had the right to free speech. Most Americans were Protestant Christians, but there were also many people of other religions, including Roman Catholics, Mormons and Jews.

STRONG BELIEFS

Native Americans, who had been turned off their lands, and black families descended from slaves, did not enjoy this equality. But many drew strength from their religious beliefs. In the late 1800s large numbers of Native Americans joined the Ghost Dance movement, taking part in ceremonies that called on the spirits of dead ancestors to help them reclaim their land.

Many black Americans were Christians. They expressed their hardship, and their trust in God, in moving songs called spirituals. Sometimes traditional African beliefs mingled with their Christian faith. This also happened in South America and the Caribbean. There, Christianity, Native American religious ideas and African beliefs joined to create new forms of worship.

► This American travel poster shows the Statue of Liberty against a dark New York sky, with the lights of the city's skyscrapers shining in the background.

ZIONISM

MIDDLE EAST

Zionists were Jewish people from Europe, America and Asia, who wanted to create a homeland in Palestine, where Jews had lived thousands of years earlier. Their campaigns led to fighting with other Middle Eastern peoples. These included the Muslim and Christian inhabitants of Palestine, and the leaders of nearby kingdoms, who wanted to create a non-religious, Arabic-speaking state. The Jewish nation of Israel was finally created in 1948.

SAUDI ARABIA

Saudi Arabia was created by people who wanted a homeland where their Muslim faith could be expressed. Between 1902 and 1925, Abd al-Aziz ibn Saud, a member of an old princely family, took control of most of Arabia by settling over 200 religious communities there. Their members farmed the land, organized armies, and made sure Muslim religious laws were kept. They faced opposition from less religious states. But Sharia (Muslim holy law) still rules Saudi Arabia today.

RELIGIOUS BELIEFS

AFRICA

There were many types of African religion, but most worshippers shared several major beliefs. They believed in a great creator god and prayed to many lesser gods, too. They also believed in spirits that could help or harm. These could be the souls of dead ancestors, or the 'living force' that flowed through the natural world.

From the 1850s onwards, Christian missionaries were active in many African countries. As well as teaching their faith, they provided medical care and education. North Africa remained mostly Muslim, as it had been for centuries. But elsewhere, various forms of Christianity existed alongside traditional African beliefs.

MAHATMA GANDHI

SOUTH ASIA

Most Indian people were Hindus, but there were also Muslims, Sikhs, Buddhists, Parsees and Jains. Many put their religious differences aside to campaign for freedom from British rule. The greatest Indian leader, Mohandas Gandhi, was inspired by his Hindu faith to use only non-violent methods in the fight. He encouraged followers to use 'truth weapons', such as prayer meetings, hunger strikes and silent sit-down protests. Gandhi inspired such respect that he was called 'Mahatma', meaning 'Great Soul'.

Sadly, after India became independent in 1947, fighting broke out between Hindus and Muslims, and millions of people were killed. Gandhi was murdered by a fellow-Hindu, who thought he was too friendly with people of other faiths.

◄ The great Indian independence campaigner Gandhi on a visit to London in 1931, to meet government leaders.

▲ Japanese kamikaze pilots were inspired by National Shinto ideas. They bravely flew suicide missions against enemy battleships.

NATIONAL SHINTO

EAST ASIA

In the late 1800s traditional Japanese beliefs continued. One Japanese leader summed up what he thought was best for his country in the slogan: 'Eastern ethics, Western science'. From 1890 onwards, the Japanese government encouraged the growth of a new religion, called National Shinto. It combined ancient Japanese beliefs about gods and spirits with hero-worship of the Japanese emperor, and the feeling that the Japanese people were best. Samurai warrior values of bravery, loyalty and self-discipline were also included in this faith. At first, National Shinto inspired noble behaviour. But in the 1930s and 1940s, when Japan was at war, Japanese leaders also used it to justify cruelty to non-Japanese.

MISSIONARY WORK

AUSTRALASIA

European settlers brought their Christian faith to Australia, New Zealand and the Pacific Islands. They also encouraged Christian missionaries to work among local peoples, in the hope that they would give up their traditional beliefs. The Australian government even introduced a 'White Australia' policy. It assumed that Aboriginal people, their beliefs and ideas, would soon be wiped out by 'progress' and a Western way of life.

THE DREAMTIME

In Australia, religious beliefs were centred on the Dreamtime, a long-ago era when the ancestors of all living creatures danced on the Earth. In New Zealand, Maori people also honoured the spirits of dead ancestors, and believed that the gods had blessed certain people and places with magic powers. For many years, few white Australians respected these ancient beliefs. But towards the end of Einstein's life, some began to understand their importance, and to treat them with respect.

▼ This bark painting was made by Australian Aboriginal artist Milingibi.

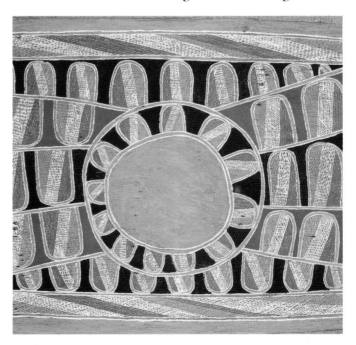

GLOSSARY

alliance A friendly agreement between nations or peoples.

ally A friendly person or nation.

antibiotic A drug that kills bacteria (microscopic organisms that can cause disease).

apartheid The South African government policy that was designed to keep people of different races apart. It took away many of black people's rights.

Art Deco A style of art, popular in the 1930s, known for its linear and angular designs.

atheist A person who does not believe in God.

atom one of the tiny particles that make up matter.

atomic bomb A weapon that splits atoms to create an extremely hot, powerful explosion. This gives off deadly, invisible rays.

aviator An aeroplane pilot.

Bakelite An early form of plastic that was hard, brittle and shiny.

batik A technique used to print cloth. Wax is applied to some areas of the cloth before it is dyed. The dye then colours only the unwaxed areas, creating a pattern.

Bauhaus A famous art college in Germany that encouraged modern, industrial-style designs.

black hole A part of space where gravity is so strong that no light can escape.

blues American popular songs, often with sad words about love or poverty.

Bolshevik One of the extreme Communists who played a part in the Russian Revolution of 1917.

Buddhism A religion based on the teachings of Prince Siddhartha Gautama, who lived in India around 550 BC.

capitalism A political system that encourages private ownership of land, homes and businesses.

ceramic Made from baked clay.

Charleston An energetic American dance with fast, complicated footwork.

Christian A person who believes in the teachings of Jesus Christ, a religious teacher who lived in the Middle East around 30 AD.

civil rights The rights of citizens, usually including the right to vote, receive an education, have a job, marry, and follow one's religion.

civil servants Officials in government departments.

civil war A war between rival groups within one country.

civilian A person who is not a member of the armed forces.

Cold War The period of tension between the USA and other non-Communist Western nations, and the USSR that lasted from 1947 to 1991.

collective farm A vast farm that is owned by the state.

colony A country ruled by a stronger foreign state.

Communism A system of government in which the state runs everything and nobody owns private property.

dictator A political leader who takes complete control of a country and rules alone.

empire A large area of land, including several different nations or peoples, governed by a single ruler called an emperor.

gramophone An early form of record player.

gravity The invisible force that pulls objects towards one another.

guerrilla A soldier who uses surprise tactics to fight against a stronger, better organized army.

Hindu A person who follows the Hindu religion, which grew up in India between 1500 and 600 BC.

Holocaust The mass murder of Jews, gipsies and others by Adolf Hitler's Nazi party.

homo erectus An extinct species of early people who lived from about 1.5 million to 300,000 years ago.

immigrant A person who moves to another country to live.

Impressionism A style of painting that creates images by using patterns of colour, light and shade.

irrigation Bringing water to dry land along specially built channels so that crops can grow there.

Islam The religion preached by Muhammad, a prophet who lived in Arabia from 570-632 AD. It teaches that there is only one God, called Allah. Followers of Islam are called Muslims.

Jain A person who follows the teachings of a group of ancient Indian religious teachers. Jains try not to harm any living creatures, and to live pure, simple lives.

Jews Descendants of the people who lived in Judah (parts of present-day Israel, Palestine, Syria and Jordan) around 1000 BC, and who later settled in many parts of the world. Jewish people follow the religion of Judaism and observe many traditional customs.

kamikaze A Japanese pilot who dive-bombed US warships during the Second World War, knowing that he would die on his mission.
kibbutz (plural **kibbutzim**) A communal farm in Israel.

locomotive An engine that pulls railway trains.

mandate An order or command.
matter The material from which everything in the universe is made. Matter itself is made up of tiny particles called atoms.
merino A breed of sheep that produces fine, silky wool.
missionary A person who tries to convert others to their own religious beliefs.
Morse Code A code made up of long and short sounds (or flashes of light) that spell out letters and words. It is used to send messages.

nationalism Pride in and loyalty to one's country.
Nazism The beliefs of Nazis (members of the National Socialist German Workers' Party), who ruled Germany from 1933 to 1945. Nazis wanted to make Germany great, conquer more territory, and remove all non-Germans from their land.
Nobel Prize An important award, given to people who have made outstanding contributions to science, medicine or world peace.

pacifist A person who believes that war is morally wrong.
paper A published lecture or essay.
Parsee A person who follows the teachings of Zoroaster, a religious thinker who lived in Persia in about the 7th century BC.
pasteurization Heating food or medicines to destroy germs.
plantation A big farm, planted with just one kind of crop.
Prohibition The period of US history (1920-1933) during which the sale of alcohol was banned.
propaganda Information that gives a one-sided view.
property dealer A person who buys and sells houses and land.
Protestants Christians who belong to churches that broke away from the Roman Catholic Church in the sixteenth century.

Qing The dynasty that ruled China from 1644 to 1912.
quasar A very remote, bright object far away in space that sends out radiation as well as light.

rabies A deadly disease passed on by bites from infected animals.
racism Unfair treatment of people on the grounds of race.
radioactive Emitting invisible rays.
Raj The lifestyle and political ideas of the British people who ruled India from 1857 to 1947.
rayon The world's first synthetic fibre, made from wood pulp and acid. It was invented in 1884.
republican A person who supports a system of government in which leaders are elected by ordinary people, and there are no kings, queens or emperors.
Roman Catholic A Christian who belongs to the church led by the Pope in Rome.

samurai An ancient Japanese warrior who followed a strict code of honour and bravery.
Sharia Muslim law, which is based on the teachings of the Qur'an, the Muslim holy book.
Sikh A follower of the Indian religion founded by Guru Nanak in the sixteenth century. It teaches belief in one god.
soviet The Russian word for 'council'. After 1917, it was used by Communists to describe the group that governed the USSR.
spiritual A religious song, often based on words from the Bible.
sub-continent A large land mass smaller than a continent. The Indian subcontinent contains modern India, Pakistan, Nepal, and Bangladesh.
Surrealism A style of art that creates distorted, dream-like images of people and objects.
synthetic Made in laboratories or factories rather than in nature.

transistor A miniature device used to carry electric current.
tsar The title used by the emperors of Russia.

welfare state A country that provides benefits for citizens who are old, unemployed or ill.
woodcut A picture created by carving a design in wood, covering the design in ink, then pressing paper on top.

X-rays Rays that can pass through flesh and clothes. They are often used to produce images of bones and other parts of the body.

Zionist A person who campaigned for a new nation to be created where Jewish people could live.

INDEX